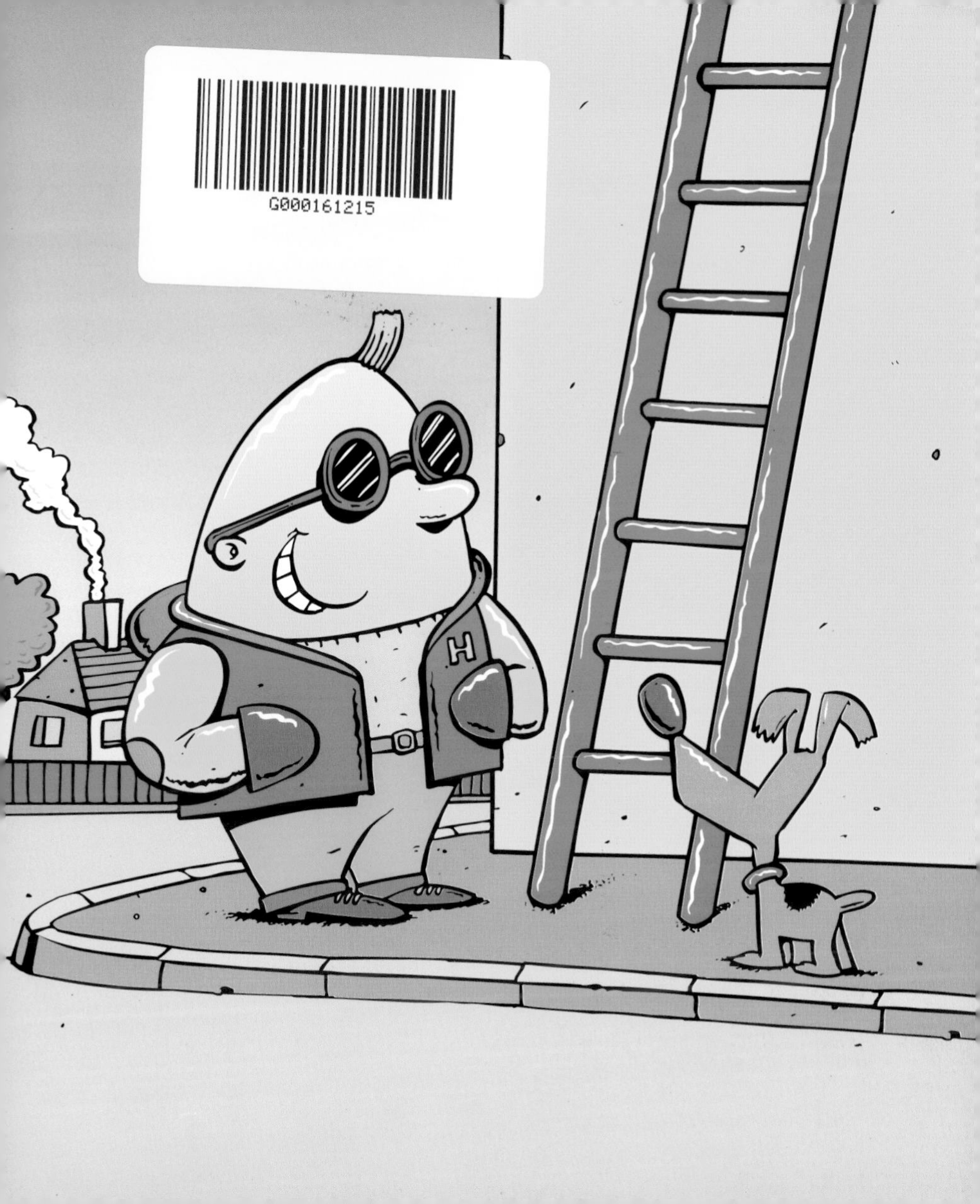
H

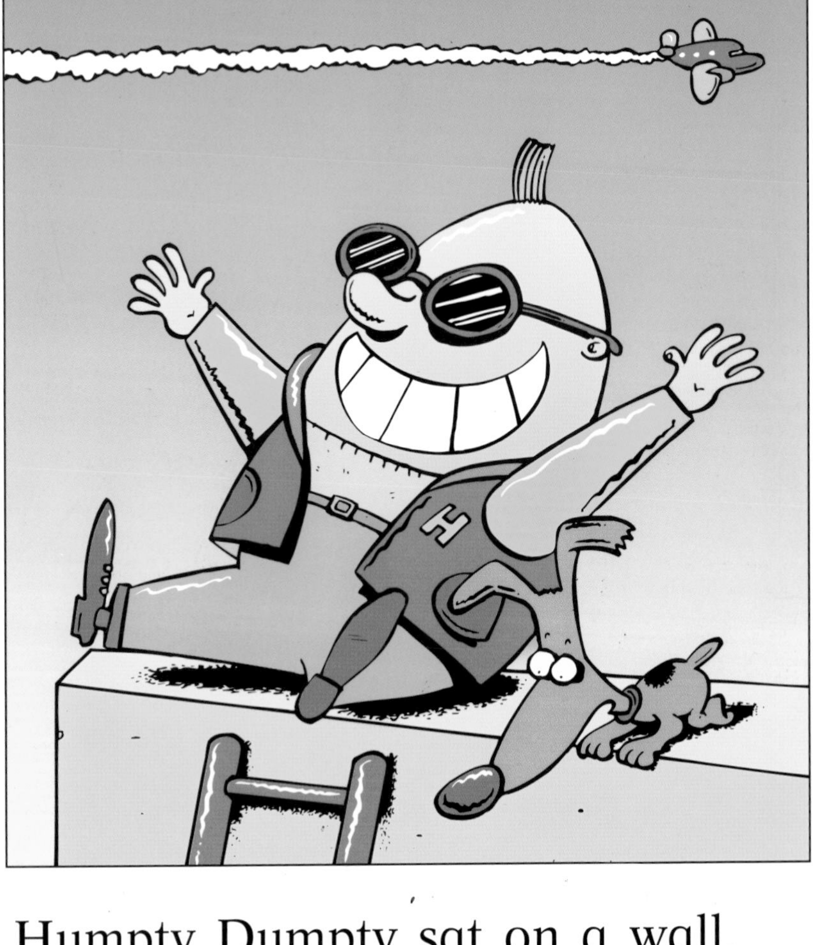

Humpty Dumpty sat on a wall.

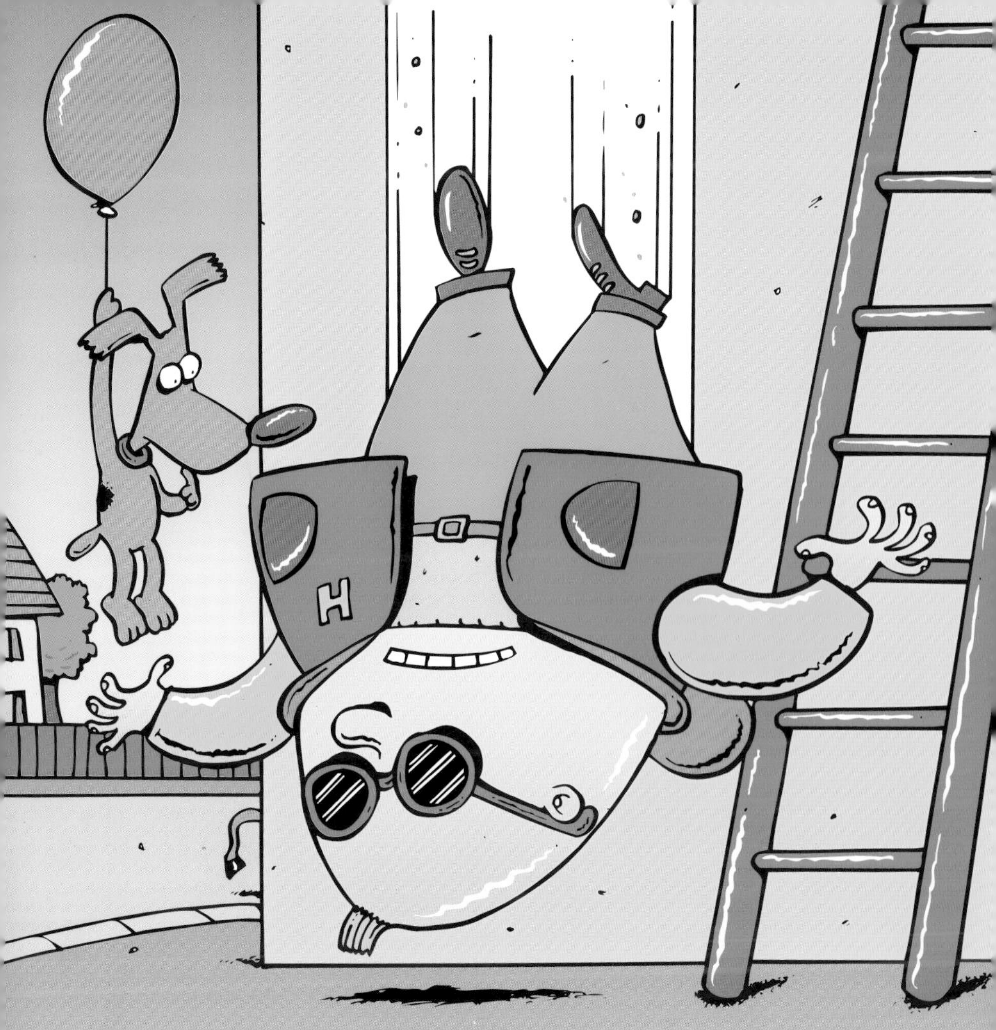

Humpty Dumpty had a great fall.

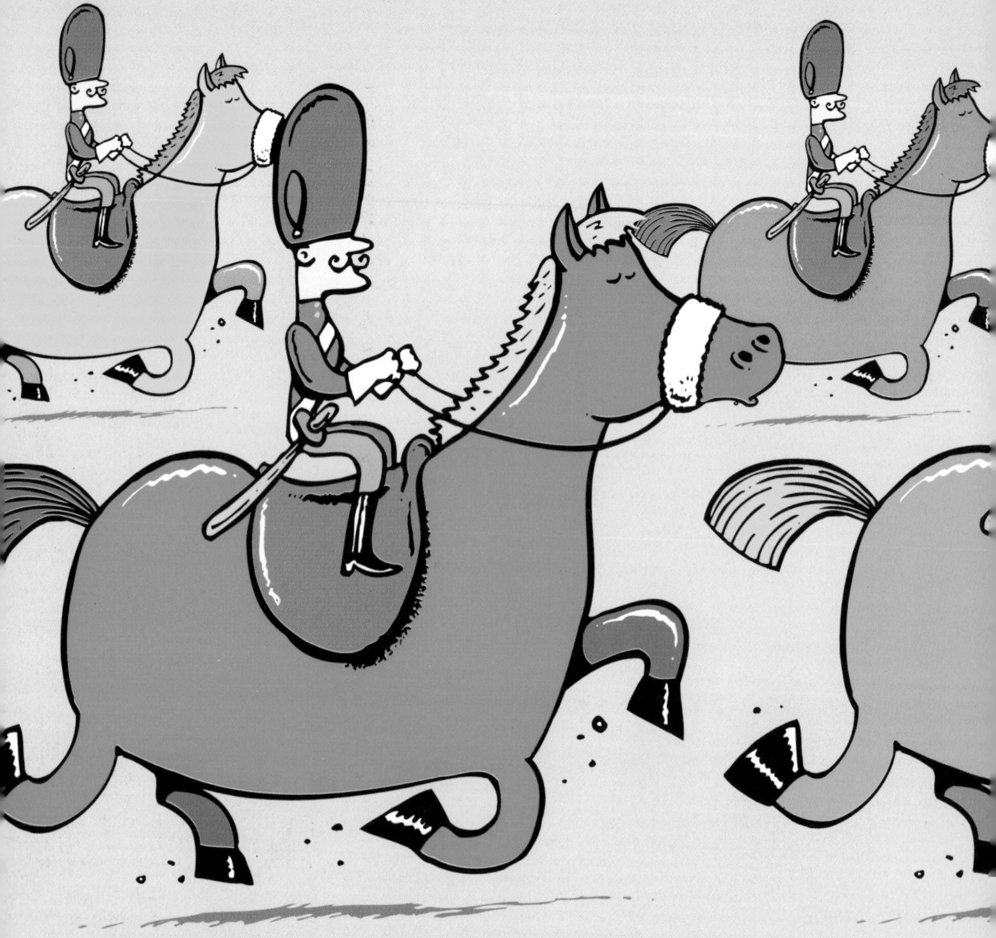

All the king's horses,

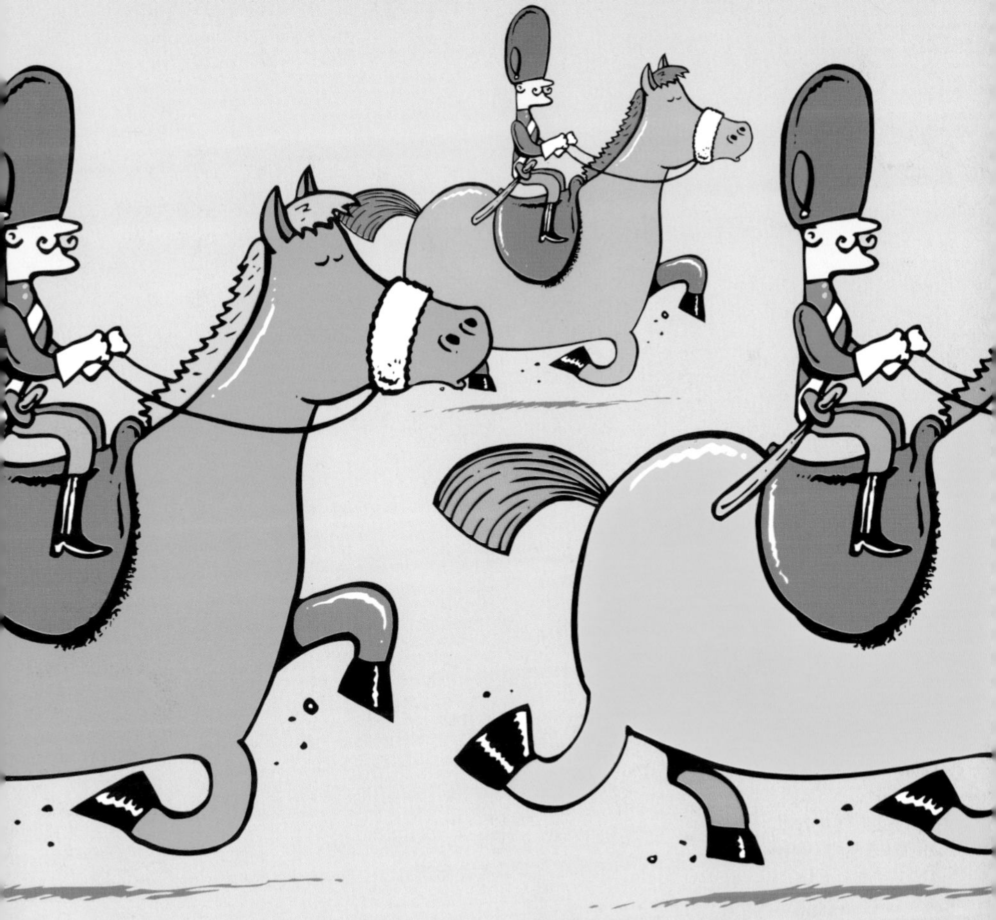

and all the king's men,

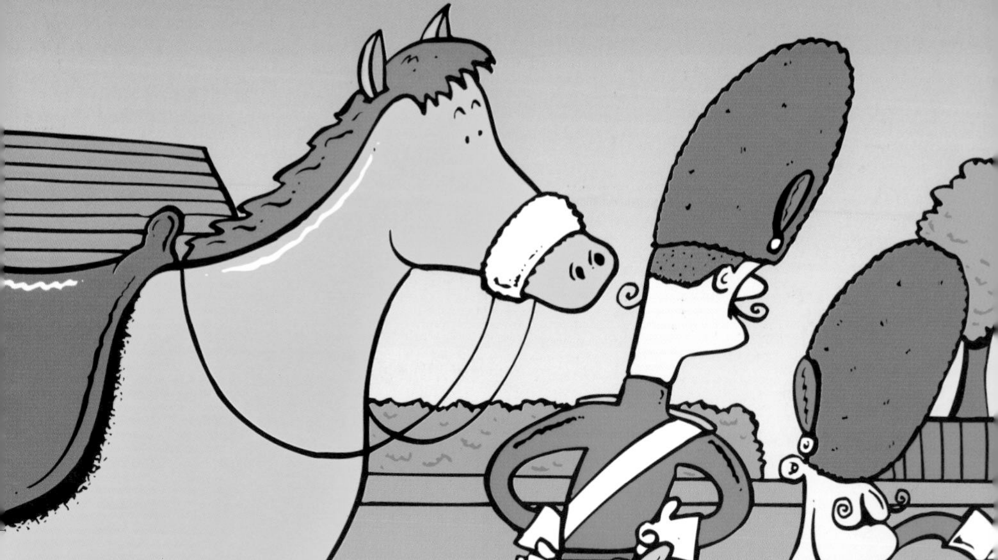

couldn't put Humpty together again.

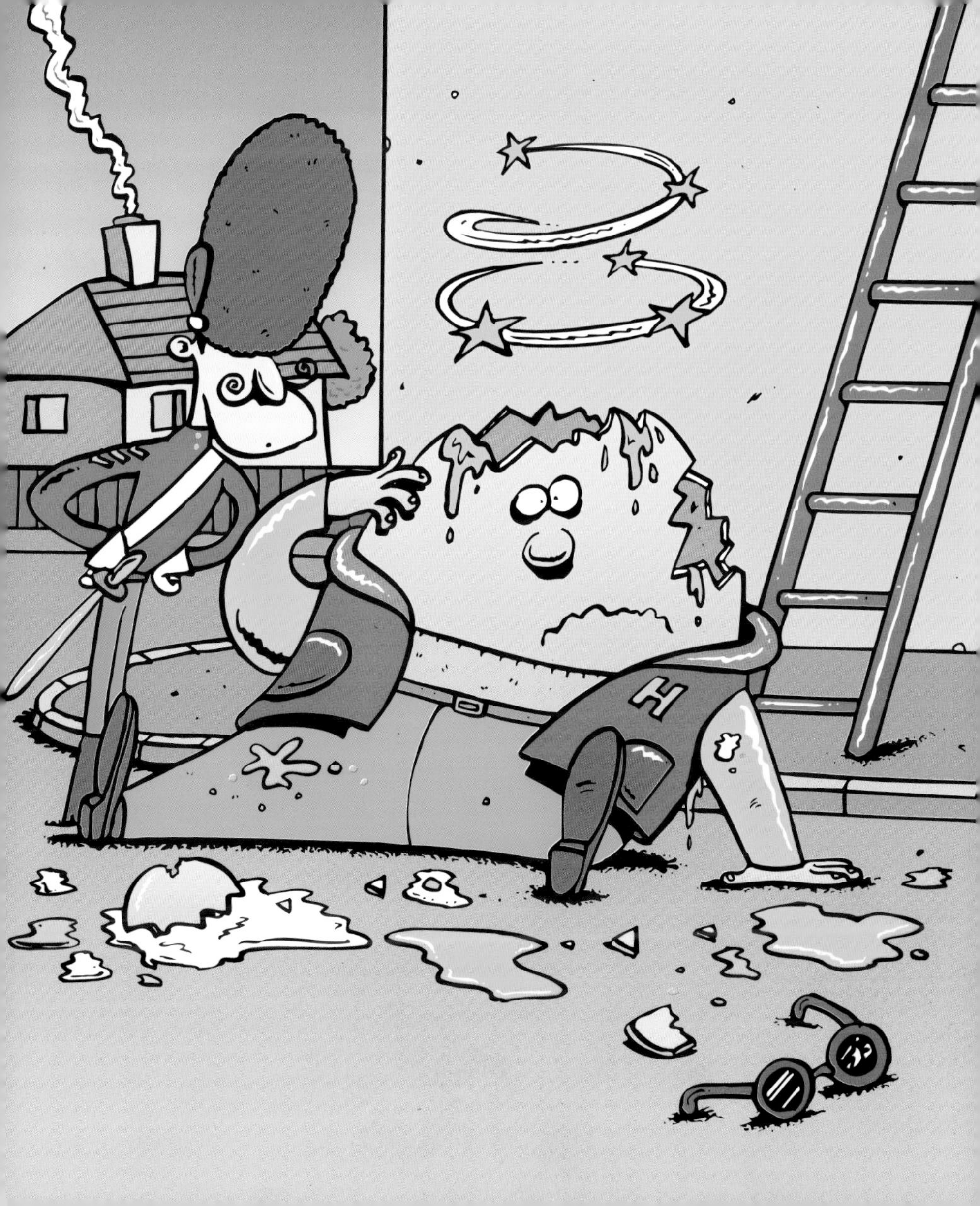

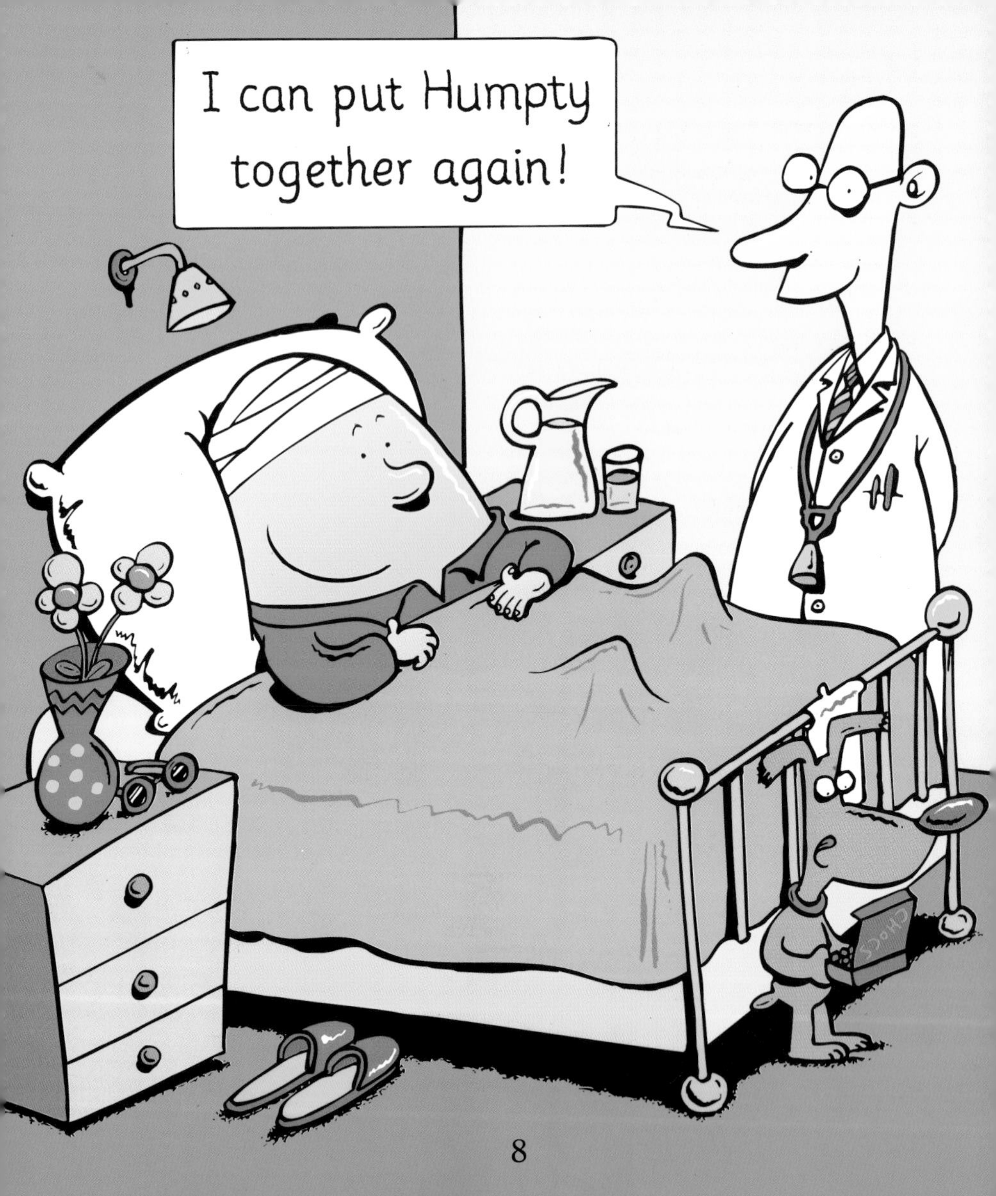
I can put Humpty together again!
CHOCS